WITHDRAWN

RANDY ORTON

A LIVING LEGACY

by Martin Gitlin

Consultant:
Mike Johnson, Writer
PWInsider.com

CAPSTONE PRESS
a capstone imprint

Velocity is published by Capstone Press,
1710 Roe Crest Drive, North Mankato, Minnesota 56003.
www.capstonepub.com

Library of Congress Cataloging-in-Publication Data
Gitlin, Marty.
 Randy Orton : a living legacy / by Martin Gitlin.
 p. cm.—(Pro wrestling stars)
 Includes bibliographical references and index.
 Summary: "Describes the life of Randy Orton, both in and out of the ring"—Provided
by publisher.
 ISBN 978-1-4296-8675-4 (library binding)
 ISBN 978-1-62065-361-6 (ebook pdf)
 1. Orton, Randy—Juvenile literature. 2. Wrestlers—United States—Biography—Juvenile
literature. I. Title.
GV1196.O77G58 2013
796.812092—dc23 [B]   2012011304

Editorial Credits
Mandy Robbins, editor; Sarah Bennett, designer; Laura Manthe, production specialist

Photo Credits
Corbis: Bettmann, 10; Getty Images: Ethan Miller, 27, WireImage/Kevin Mazur Archive,
24, WireImage/KMazur, 33 (middle), 37 (top), WireImage/Ray Mickshaw, 40; iStockphotos:
grimgram, 12; Newscom: Carlos Milanes, 31, Splash News/Heather Rousseau, 38 (top), Splash
News/Titomedia, 18, WENN Photos CD1, 30, 45, WENN Photos DR2, 39, WENN Photos
SI1, 7, ZUMA Press, 5, 16, 19, 21, 35, ZUMA Press/Globe Photos, 28 (top), ZUMA Press/
Panoramic, 20, 22, ZUMA Press/UPN-TV/WWF, 28 (bottom); Photo by Wrealano@aol.com,
13; Shutterstock: Anastasios Kandris, 25 (inset), Andreas Meyer, 14-15 (snake), Chyrko Olena,
32, 33, 34, 35 (poster), ella1977 (camouflage), 11, Fortunepig78, 32 (fist), JungleOutThere,
41 (stroller), karlovserg, 34 (handcuffs), koya979, 14 (gravestone), Left Eyed Photography,
29, Lusoimages, 44, Pablo77, 15 (lion), PILart, 11 (tags), RetroClipArt, 41 (hand), shutswis,
37 (tacks), SSylenko, 9, Tsurukame Design, 38 (casket); Wikimedia: Fatima, cover, 1
(background), Shamsuddin Muhammad, cover

Artistic Effects
Shutterstock

Printed in the United States of America in Stevens Point, Wisconsin.
032012   006678WZF12

TABLE OF CONTENTS

INTRODUCTION

PRO WRESTLING POWERHOUSE

TAKING ON A PUNK

On April 3, 2011, more than 71,000 fans packed the Georgia Dome in Atlanta. They were there to witness the biggest pro wrestling event of the year—*WrestleMania*. The crowd noise rose to a booming roar when the announcer introduced Randy Orton.

Randy began his long walk down the aisle to the wrestling ring amid music and smoke. Flashing lights lit up the stadium. Randy's injured right leg was wrapped up in athletic tape, but he still managed to swagger toward the mat. His trademark glare was on his face as well. As he neared the ring, Randy shot a menacing look at his opponent, CM Punk.

RANDY ORTON

HEIGHT
6 feet, 5 inches (196 centimeters)

WEIGHT
235 pounds (107 kilograms)

NICKNAMES
Legend Killer, The Viper, Apex Predator

SIGNATURE MOVES
DDT, RKO

CM PUNK

HEIGHT
6 ft, 2 in (188 cm)

WEIGHT
218 lbs (99 kg)

NICKNAMES
Second City Savior, Straight Edge Superstar

SIGNATURE MOVES
Anaconda Vise, G.T.S.

The two men squared off, and the match began. Punk showed no mercy. He went after Randy's bad leg time and time again. For a while, it seemed like Randy was going to go down. But just when it looked like the end was near, Randy found his inner strength. He sent CM Punk to the ground with his signature move, the RKO. The match was over, and Randy Orton had once again proven his power in the wrestling ring.

Randy Orton (right), attempts to slam CM Punk's head into the ropes during their match on April 3, 2011.

WORKING UP THE CROWD

Millions of fans have cheered and booed for Randy over the years. Sometimes he's a **babyface**, and other times he's a **heel**. Either way, Randy tries to get the audience involved in his matches. He doesn't talk as much as other wrestlers, but his facial expressions speak volumes. The glare in his eyes shows that he means business. The cocky smirk on his face says more than any villain's evil laugh. Randy's tough-guy attitude fires up the crowd. His aggressive style of wrestling sometimes includes the use of makeshift weapons. Chairs are one of his favorite objects with which to beat opponents.

babyface—a wrestler who acts as a hero in the ring

heel—a wrestler who acts as a villain in the ring

WHaT RandY SaID:

"I can get 10,000 people to boo me if I drop a guy with a clothesline and drop my knee on the back of his head with a smirk. And then it's like 'aww, boo' and you get with it," he says. "My goal is to get the best, or worst, reaction from them as I can."

FACT

Orton has joined his fellow World Wrestling Entertainment (WWE) wrestlers for shows all over the world. "The crowds [overseas] aren't used to seeing us live, so they go crazy, which makes it all more exciting," he says.

CHAPTER 1
GROWING UP ORTON

April fools! Randy Orton was born on April 1, 1980. At that time Randy's father, Bob Orton Jr., and uncle Barry Orton held the International Championship Wrestling (ICW) Southeastern Tag Team belt. Randy's grandfather Bob Orton Sr. also enjoyed a career as a professional wrestler. Check out the details of Randy's impressive family tree.

BECKY (SISTER)

BOB ORTON SR. (GRANDFATHER)

The Orton wrestling tradition began with Bob Orton Sr. He was known as The Big O and El Lobo. He battled pro wrestling legends such as Lou Thesz and Bruno Sammartino. The eldest Orton wrestler began his career at a time when wrestlers traveled all over the United States. He teamed up with his son Bob Jr. to win the Florida Tag Team title in 1976. In 2006, a week before he died, Bob Sr. marveled at how Randy's aggressive style in the ring was just like his own.

BOB ORTON JR. (FATHER)

Randy's dad was best known as Cowboy Bob Orton. He wore his trademark cowboy hat and boots. Cowboy Bob wrestled his way into the WWE Hall of Fame. Until 2002, WWE was called the World Wrestling Federation (WWF). Cowboy Bob gained his greatest fame in the 1980s as a heel with the WWF. Cowboy Bob **feuded** with the most famous wrestlers of his time, including Hulk Hogan, "Rowdy" Roddy Piper, and Andre the Giant.

RANDY

NATHAN (BROTHER)

Randy's brother Nathan also has a career in the ring. But this ring has eight sides. Nathan Orton has made a name for himself in the sport of **mixed martial arts**. These fighters face off in an octagon-shaped ring.

COWBOY BOB (FATHER) + ELAINE ORTON (MOTHER)

BARRY ORTON (UNCLE)

Barry Orton was known in the ring as Superstar Barry O and Zodiac. He won several titles in regional wrestling programs. But Barry never gained the same fame in the ring as his wrestling relatives. He later became an actor and director under the name of Barrymore Barlow. Barry is also a skilled musician. He plays the drums, guitar, and piano. He once joined the band Steppenwolf on stage to play the legendary rock-and-roll song, "Born To Be Wild."

feud—to have a long-running quarrel between two people or groups of people

mixed martial arts—a full-combat sport combining wrestling and martial arts moves

BOB ORTON SR.

GROWING UP AND GROWING BIG

Randy became friends with many wrestlers years before he tangled with them in the ring. His father often brought home his coworkers. André the Giant, "Rowdy" Roddy Piper, and Greg "The Hammer" Valentine were frequent visitors to the Orton home. Randy also traveled around the country to watch his dad in action. At 5 years old, he watched his father knock out "Mr. Wonderful" Paul Orndorff at the very first *WrestleMania*.

André the Giant throws Mike Adams during the World Battle Royal wrestling match in 1977.

It was clear that wrestling was in Randy's blood at an early age. He was eager to develop his own wrestling skills. As a kid, Randy competed in a youth wrestling league. He went on to become one of the top wrestlers in Missouri. He was so talented that he earned a spot in the Danny Hodge World High School Championships.

After high school, Randy had a strong desire to enter pro wrestling. But his father tried to talk him out of it. Bob Jr. knew it meant a lot of traveling and time spent away from family. Randy agreed to join the Marines instead. But he couldn't control his rebellious spirit. Randy disobeyed orders and went **AWOL** twice. This landed Randy in a military jail. He was given a dishonorable discharge.

AWOL—to leave or be absent from one's military duties without permission

CHAPTER 2

CLIMBING THE LADDER OF SUCCESS

Randy began his pro wrestling training with the Mid-Missouri Wrestling Association. Among his instructors was none other than his father. Randy showed enough talent to earn a contract with the WWE. WWE officials sent him for further training with Ohio Valley Wrestling (OVW) in 2000.

OVW TRAINING

Training with OVW is divided into beginning and advanced sessions. Instructors teach wrestlers how to safely perform various holds and moves. Classes last for three hours at a time. By the end everyone is soaked in sweat.

But the OVW doesn't just teach the physical part of pro wrestling. Students there also learn the psychology of the sport. The psychology courses help wrestlers learn proper timing when it comes to their story lines.

John Cena strikes a pose when he was known as the Prototype.

Randy had to work his way up to being in the ring with WWE superstars. He beat Mr. Black on February 14, 2001, and defeated Flash Flanagan three months later. Both matches resulted in Randy earning Hardcore Champion crowns. *Pro Wrestling Illustrated* named Randy the Rookie of the Year in 2001. After such an impressive year, WWE officials thought he was ready for the big time.

Randy made his WWE TV **debut** on April 25, 2002, against long-time wrestler Hardcore Holly. Randy was nearly pinned, but he rolled Holly over and pinned him for the win.

debut—a peron's first public appearance

CHAPTER 3
THE ORTON IMAGE

As Randy has grown in his career, his image has changed. Nowhere has this been more apparent than in his nicknames. Check out some of the names Randy has been known by throughout the years.

LEGEND KILLER

When Randy joined the WWE in 2002, he was much younger than many of his competitors. Randy started out as a babyface. He became known for beating long-time heels such as Mick Foley, Jake "The Snake" Roberts, and Sargeant Slaughter. Randy soon earned the nickname "The Legend Killer." But it wasn't long before The Legend Killer turned heel himself. Randy spit in the face of 60-year-old Harley Race. He also attacked 80-year-old female champion Fabulous Moolah.

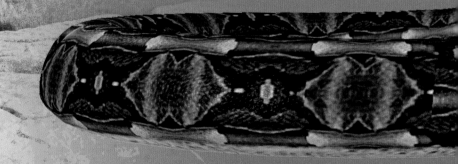

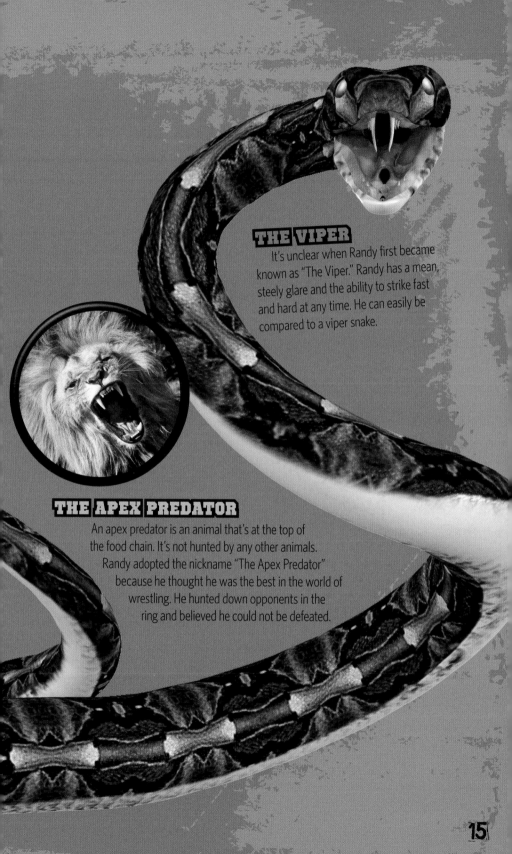

THE VIPER

It's unclear when Randy first became known as "The Viper." Randy has a mean, steely glare and the ability to strike fast and hard at any time. He can easily be compared to a viper snake.

THE APEX PREDATOR

An apex predator is an animal that's at the top of the food chain. It's not hunted by any other animals. Randy adopted the nickname "The Apex Predator" because he thought he was the best in the world of wrestling. He hunted down opponents in the ring and believed he could not be defeated.

WHAT DID HE JUST SAY?

"I'm a one-man dynasty!"

How does Randy get fans rocking when he's not in the ring? He opens his big mouth. Some of the things he says are cocky, some are rude, and some are just plain outrageous. Randy loves to brag about his talent. And he doesn't shy away from a challenge. Check out some of the wild statements made by Randy Orton through the years.

"I'm here to tell everyone about my new show called 'Orton Knows Best.'"

"My accomplishments are endless."

"I would RKO my own grandmother to keep hold of this championship. Then I would RKO your grandmother just to see the look on her face."

"Greatness has entered the ring. Thank you very much, you may bow at will."

"I entered this ring Randy Orton, legend killer. When all was said and done, I left as Randy Orton, legend."

"Not only am I better looking ... I'm just plain better."

FACT

When Randy is feeling nasty, he has been known to spit on his opponents. He caused quite a stir by spitting on the faces of legends Mick Foley and Harley Race.

RANDY'S INK

One way Randy has shown his growth as a person has been through his tattoos. The tattoos Randy had done in 2008 had more meaning to his life than those drawn earlier.

EARLY TATTOOS

Randy placed tribal tattoos all over his body early in his wrestling career. "The tribal work I had before had no meaning behind it," he admitted.

Randy had a tattoo that read "USMC" on his left arm as a tribute to the Marines. He later covered this tattoo with others.

In 2008 Randy decided to get some tattoos that did have meaning to him. After getting married and having a daughter, Randy added tattoos that showed his pride in becoming a husband and father. His wife's name, Samantha, is tattooed on his right forearm.

One of Randy's tattoos features a Bible verse. It reads: "Be sober, be vigilant, because your adversary the devil, as a roaring lion walketh about seeking whom he may devour." He said that the verse is true to his heart.

Randy's rose tattoo symbolizes his love for daughter Alanna. Her name and birth date is displayed on his left arm in Roman numerals.

Randy has a series of skulls running down his arms.

FACT

It took 40 to 50 hours for Randy to get all his new tattoos inked on his body.

CHAPTER 4
MAJOR MOVES

Having grown up in the business, pro wrestling moves come easy to Randy. He is a very technically sound wrestler. Randy uses a wide variety of moves to overpower his opponents.

INVERTED HEADLOCK BACKBREAKER

One of Randy's crushing moves is the Inverted Headlock Backbreaker. Standing back-to-back with his opponent, Randy puts his arm around the opponent's neck in a headlock. He then twists the opponent's neck and falls to his knees. The opponent ends up arched over Randy's back.

EUROPEAN UPPERCUT

When Randy needs a short, quick move to send his opponent to the mat, he uses the European Uppercut. He simply smashes his massive forearm into the opponent's chin.

BODY SCISSORS WITH CHINLOCK

There is no escape when Randy uses this double move. The body scissors is applied when Randy squeezes an opponent with his powerful legs. The grip tightens as Randy squeezes his hands around the opponent's chin.

GUTWRENCH ELEVATED NECKBREAKER

Randy displays his brute strength with the Gutwrench Elevated Neckbreaker. When his opponent is hunched over, Randy wraps his arms around the opponent's stomach and flips him onto his shoulders. Randy then falls to a sitting position while his opponent crashes to the mat.

WHEELBARROW SUPLEX

Randy doesn't need an actual wheelbarrow to perform the Wheelbarrow Suplex. He stands behind an opponent and wraps his arms around the opponent's waist. Then he falls backward. Randy lands gently, but his opponent doesn't. Randy flings him to the mat with great force.

21

FINISHING TOUCHES

A finishing move often helps define a wrestler. It is also called a signature move. Though Randy has used various moves to defeat his opponents, the "RKO" has brought him the most fame. Randy takes opponents and fans by surprise with this move because he performs it quickly. When the RKO is used, the match is usually over.

Randy uses the RKO on Christian.

RKO

Randy begins this move by grabbing the neck of his opponent. Then he leaps sideways, sometimes off the top rope. He falls forward, pulling his foe down with him and slamming his head to the mat. In 2010 Randy leaped high enough to yank Chris Jericho off the middle of a ladder for an RKO!

RUNNING PUNT KICK TO THE HEAD

To perform a Running Punt Kick to the Head, Randy runs forward and kicks a kneeling opponent in the head. Randy gave WWE Chairman of the Board Vince McMahon a Running Punt Kick to the Head in January 2009.

FALLING CLOTHESLINE

Randy uses a Falling Clothesline to hang opponents out to dry. He runs forward with an outstretched arm. Then he falls into his foe, ramming his arm into the opponent. The move can be applied while the opponent is standing or lying flat on the mat.

DDT

One of Randy's most interesting moves is the DDT. He wraps his arm around an opponent's neck. The opponent's feet balance on the ropes so that his body is **horizontal** at Randy's waist. Randy then drops down while his opponent falls to the mat.

horizontal—flat and parallel to the ground

CHAPTER 5
SHOWDOWNS!

The best pro wrestlers are remembered for their greatest matches. They are judged by their performances with championship belts on the line. Randy has had some of the most memorable matches in WWE history.

Randy won the Intercontinental Championship belt on December 14, 2003. He defended his title until July 2004.

RANDY'S BIG WINS 1

AUGUST 15, 2004

Defending WWE World Heavyweight Champion Chris Benoit flashed his title belt in Randy's face before their 2004 showdown. But Randy soon took it away. He pinned Benoit after flattening him with an RKO. Randy cried tears of joy as he held the belt up to the crowd. He had become the youngest WWE World Heavyweight Champion in history!

OCTOBER 7, 2007

In 2007 Randy faced off against Triple H for the WWE Championship. Most of the battle took place outside the ring. Randy smashed Triple H into the steps leading to the ring. Triple H later picked up the steps and slammed them on Randy's head! By the end of the match, both men were exhausted. Somehow Randy managed to RKO Triple H onto the announcer's table. By the count of ten, Triple H still couldn't get up. Randy won the match and the title.

JUNE 15, 2009

Randy didn't just beat one opponent to win the WWE Championship for the fifth time. He beat Big Show, John Cena, and Triple H in a four-way match. Randy flattened Big Show with an RKO before pinning him to clinch the title.

CHAPTER 6

POWERFUL PARTNERS

Randy is a fierce competitor on his own. But he has also had the help of many people in the wrestling business throughout the years. Check out some of Randy's most powerful partners:

EVOLUTION

Triple H convinced Randy to join him, Ric Flair, and Batista as part of the **stable** Evolution in January 2003. The group dominated the WWE for more than a year. Little did Randy know that in the summer of 2004, his partners would turn on him. After Randy beat Chris Benoit to win the Heavyweight title, Flair, Triple H, and Batista attacked him. Randy was in no condition to fight back. But one thing was for sure—Evolution was over.

RATED-RKO

After Randy was kicked out of Evolution, he blamed Shawn Michaels and Triple H for turning his stable against him. They had been part of the stable D-Generation X. Randy's anger simmered for years. In 2006 he teamed up with Edge to form Rated-RKO. Together they worked to destroy Michaels and Triple H. Rated-RKO did just that in a tag team match one month later. But Michaels and Triple H had their revenge in January 2007 when they defeated Rated-RKO. Edge and Randy parted ways four months later.

THE LEGACY

Randy had a famous wrestling grandfather, father, and uncle. Pro wrestler Cody Rhodes' father Dusty Rhodes was a wrestling champion. So was the father of Ted DiBiase Jr. In late 2008, Randy decided to team up with Rhodes and DiBiase Jr. to create The Legacy. But DiBiase Jr. and Rhodes could not match the success of Orton, who dominated the trio. The Legacy fell apart in 2010.

Ted DiBiase Jr. (left), Randy Orton (center), and Cody Rhodes (right) presented a united front as they entered the ring during WWE's *Monday Night Raw* in August 2009.

stable—a group of wrestlers who protect each other during matches and sometimes wrestle together

MANAGING A MEAN MAN

Many pro wrestlers have managers, and Randy is no exception. Check out four people who have tackled the task of managing this mean man.

Ric Flair (left) cranks on Chris Jericho's neck at *Summerslam* in 2002.

RIC FLAIR

Randy needed guidance from an old pro when he began his WWE career. He couldn't have found a more accomplished wrestler and entertainer than Ric Flair. Flair had a flair for exciting crowds, a talent that he groomed in his student.

LITA

Lita became involved with Randy when he teamed up with Edge in 2006. She managed both of the superstars when they formed Rated-RKO. When the team broke up, Lita parted ways with Randy and stuck with Edge.

STACY KEIBLER

Stacy Keibler was more than a wrestling **diva**. Stacy managed Randy until March 2005, when he knocked her out with an RKO! At that moment, Randy went from popular face to hated heel.

FACT

In addition to being a wrestling diva, Stacy Keibler was a model and a dancer. She placed third in the hit TV reality show *Dancing With the Stars*.

COWBOY BOB ORTON

Randy's father worked as his trainer soon after Randy signed his first professional wrestling contract. Cowboy Bob also served as his manager for a short time in 2005.

diva—a female pro wrestler who may also accompany a male wrestler into the ring

CHAPTER 7
THAT HAD TO HURT!

Randy knows from experience that professional wrestling is dangerous. Randy has injured his ankle, collarbone, foot, neck, and back.

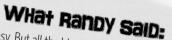

WHat RanDY SaiD:

"This isn't easy. But all the blood, sweat, tears, bruises, and the bumps you take every night that make your bones and muscles ache—it's all worth it when you walk through that curtain. There's nothing that beats it."

In an interview with the *St. Louis Post-Dispatch* in 2009, Randy reported that he had suffered six concussions during his career.

Randy separated his shoulder in a match against Brock Lesnar in 2001. He reinjured it in another match the following year.

Randy suffered a broken collarbone in 2008 in a match against Triple H. He reinjured it in a motorcycle accident later that year.

Randy has suffered from many back injuries throughout his career. This is a common ailment for pro wrestlers.

concussion—an injury to the brain caused by a hard blow to the head

CHAPTER 8

RANDY'S MOST WANTED

Rivalries are what make pro wrestling so fun. Randy has battled many WWE wrestlers. His chief rivals during the early years of his career included legends such as Ric Flair, Goldberg, Shawn Michaels, and Mick Foley. In more recent years, he has faced off with Triple H and John Cena.

WANTED
DEAD OR ALIVE

SHAWN MICHAELS was a legend. Randy was The Legend Killer. This rivalry seemed natural. Randy used brass knuckles to beat Michaels in 2003. That set the stage for other battles between Randy and Michaels, but they weren't enemies forever. In early 2005 they teamed up to beat Triple H and Ric Flair as well as Edge and Christian.

SHAWN MICHAELS

HEIGHT
6 ft, 1 in (185 cm)

WEIGHT
225 lbs (102 kg)

NICKNAME
The Heartbreak Kid (HBK)

SIGNATURE MOVE
Sweet Chin Music

RIC FLAIR helped make Randy a star. But Flair also played his part in kicking Randy out of Evolution in 2004. Flair ordered the beat down of the new champion by his Evolution teammates.

RIC FLAIR

HEIGHT
6 ft, 1 in (185 cm)

WEIGHT
243 lbs (110 kg)

NICKNAME
Nature Boy

SIGNATURE MOVE
Figure-Four Leglock

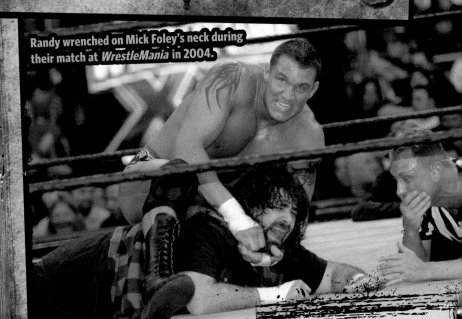

Randy wrenched on Mick Foley's neck during their match at *WrestleMania* in 2004.

Randy couldn't have shown less respect for wrestling legend **MICK FOLEY**. He spit in Foley's face. He called Foley a coward. He insulted Foley through video presentations. He attacked Foley outside the ring. These insults and attacks led to several unforgettable ring battles.

MICK FOLEY

HEIGHT
6 ft, 2 in (188 cm)

WEIGHT
287 lbs (130 kg)

NICKNAMES
Cactus Jack, Mankind

SIGNATURE MOVE
The Mandible Claw

WANTED
DEAD OR ALIVE

Randy's rivalry with **JOHN CENA** got personal in 2007. He dragged Cena's father into it. The battle began when Randy used an RKO on Cena, smashing him through a ringside chair. Cena then beat Randy for the WWE Championship. Randy dragged Cena's dad out of the stands the next day and kicked him in the head! A month later the Cenas teamed up to kick Randy in the face. Randy got back at them the next day by handcuffing the younger Cena to the ropes. Then Randy clobbered the elder Cena with another RKO.

JOHN CENA

HEIGHT
6 ft, 1 in (185 cm)

WEIGHT
251 lbs (114 kg)

NICKNAMES
Super Cena, Chain Gang Commander

SIGNATURE MOVE
Attitude Adjustment

SHERIFF

FACT
Despite their rivalry, Randy has good things to say about John Cena's skills. He thinks Cena is "light years" ahead of his fellow wrestlers on the microphone.

The feud between Randy and **TRIPLE H** reached its peak on March 9, 2009. That's when Triple H broke into Randy's house with a sledgehammer, searching for Randy. Randy came out of hiding and attacked Triple H. The two men fought in the living room, and then Triple H tossed Randy through the window!

Randy was furious about being attacked by Triple H in his own home. Later that month, Randy, Ted DiBiase Jr., and Cody Rhodes attacked Triple H in the ring. Randy handcuffed him to the ropes and took out his anger on Triple H. When Triple H's wife, Stephanie McMahon, entered the ring, Randy knocked her out with an RKO. To end the match, Randy knocked Triple H out with a sledgehammer.

FACT

Randy Orton was chosen as the Most Vicious Wrestler in the WWE in 2008.

TRIPLE H

HEIGHT
6 ft, 4 in (193 cm)

WEIGHT
255 lbs (116 kg)

NICKNAME
The Game

SIGNATURE MOVE
The Pedigree

Randy had Triple H cowering in the corner during one of their *WrestleMania* matches.

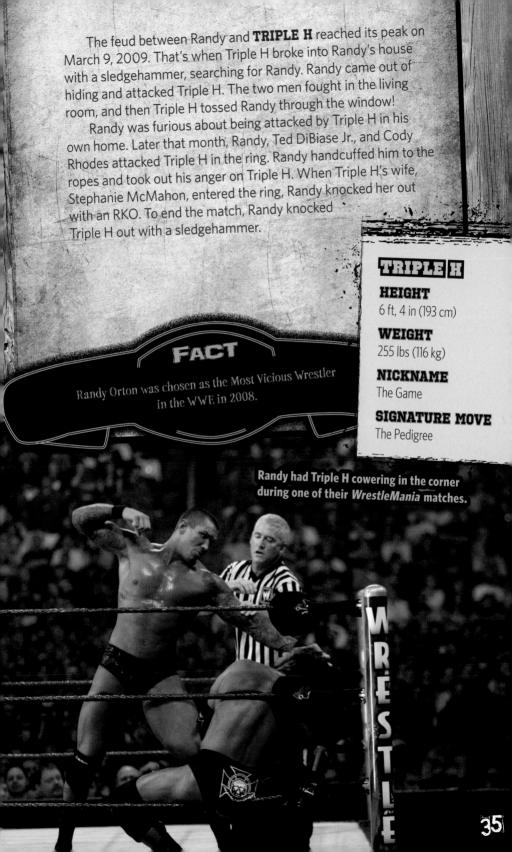

CHAPTER 9

RANDY'S WILDEST MOMENTS

Randy has one of the strongest personalities in pro wrestling. And he has always been willing to bend the rules to get what he wants. This attitude has led to some pretty wild moments. Check out some of the wildest:

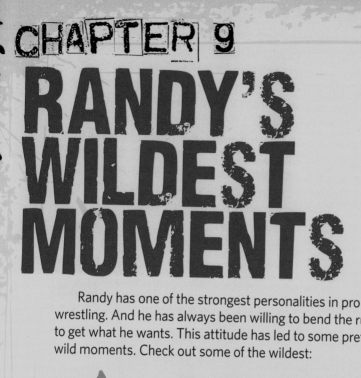

FEBRUARY 2, 2003

It was cold outside in the winter of 2003. But Randy and partner Batista made it hot for opponent Goldust. They attacked Goldust and tossed him into an electrical box. Goldust received quite the shock!

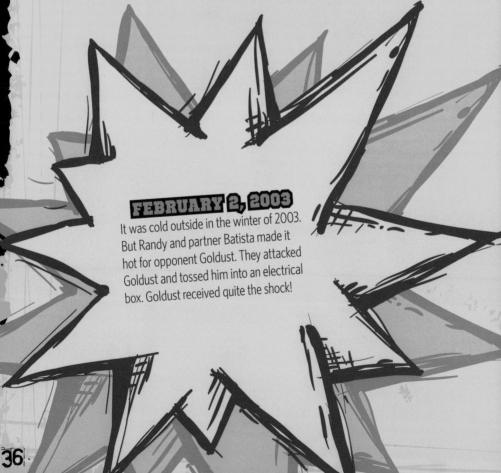

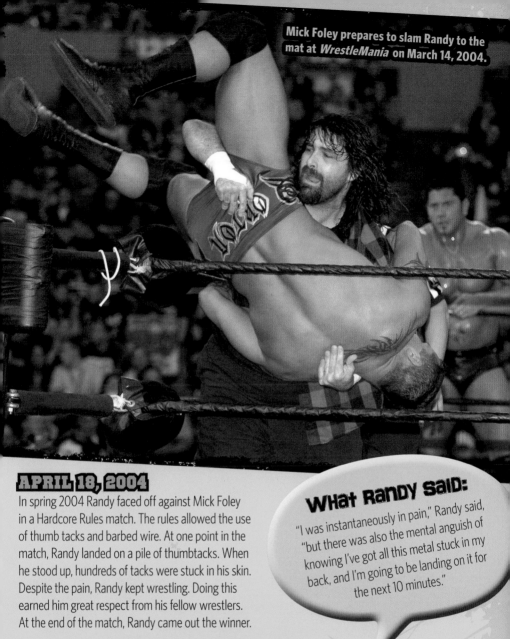

APRIL 18, 2004

In spring 2004 Randy faced off against Mick Foley in a Hardcore Rules match. The rules allowed the use of thumb tacks and barbed wire. At one point in the match, Randy landed on a pile of thumbtacks. When he stood up, hundreds of tacks were stuck in his skin. Despite the pain, Randy kept wrestling. Doing this earned him great respect from his fellow wrestlers. At the end of the match, Randy came out the winner.

WHAT RANDY SAID:

"I was instantaneously in pain," Randy said, "but there was also the mental anguish of knowing I've got all this metal stuck in my back, and I'm going to be landing on it for the next 10 minutes."

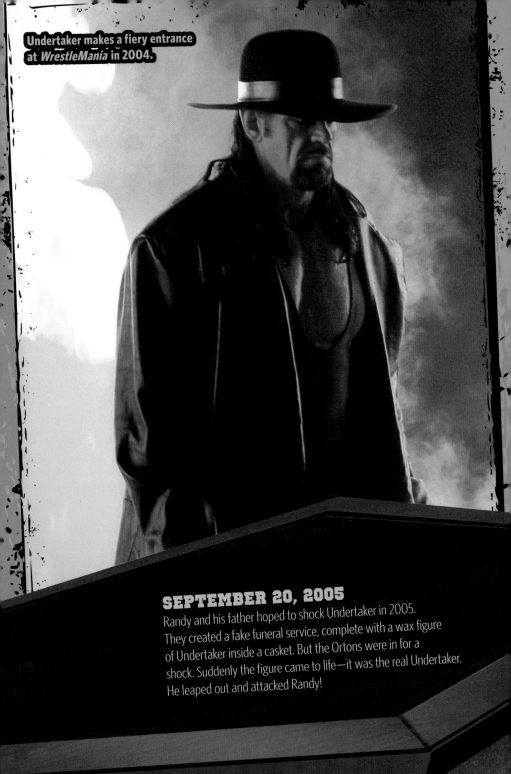

Undertaker makes a fiery entrance at *WrestleMania* in 2004.

SEPTEMBER 20, 2005

Randy and his father hoped to shock Undertaker in 2005. They created a fake funeral service, complete with a wax figure of Undertaker inside a casket. But the Ortons were in for a shock. Suddenly the figure came to life—it was the real Undertaker. He leaped out and attacked Randy!

One of the strangest story lines in Randy's career unfolded in 2006. It began when he suggested that Brooke Hogan go on a date with him. That might not have been a problem if the 18-year-old was not the daughter of legendary wrestling champion Hulk Hogan. An angry Hulk got angrier when Randy used an RKO to slam him onto a car. Hulk got his revenge by defeating Randy a month later at *Summerslam*.

Hulk Hogan and his daughter Brooke address pro wrestling fans.

JANUARY 19, 2009

An odd turn of events occurred on *Monday Night Raw* when WWE executive Stephanie McMahon was about to fire Randy. He screamed at her before she could do it. She responded by slapping him in the face. Her father Vince McMahon ordered Stephanie to leave the ring. Vince began to fire Randy, but Randy slapped him in the face before the words could leave his lips. As Vince began to rise, Randy kicked him in the head and knocked him out cold! Randy stood in disbelief at what he had done as doctors rushed in.

CHAPTER 10
LIFE OUTSIDE THE RING

Inside the ring, Randy is aggressive and intimidating. But at home he's more mellow. Randy enjoys spending time with his family.

FAMILY MAN

Randy claims to be a shy guy. Somehow he got up the nerve to ask his future wife, Samantha, for her phone number the night they met. The rest is history. They were married on September 21, 2007.

Randy towers over his wife, Samantha. He is almost a foot taller than she is.

Randy was thrilled by the birth of daughter Alanna Marie on July 12, 2008. After her birth, he said, "She is absolutely flawless from head to toe."

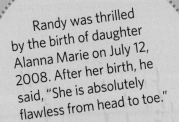

WHat RanDY SaiD:

"When I saw the little baby and when she looked up at me and heard my voice and I said, 'Wow, I made this little human being and I'm responsible for it.' I have to set a good example. I have to be a good father ... She's made me understand what life is all about."

CAN I HAVE YOUR AUTOGRAPH?

Randy tries to live as normally as possible, but sometimes his fame gets in the way. Randy recalled visiting the Six Flags St. Louis amusement park with his family. They found it hard to avoid the attention. Everywhere the family went, Randy was stopped and asked to sign autographs. The Ortons were only able to get on three or four rides in six hours.

ORTON TRIVIA

Fans know a lot about Randy the wrestler. But there's more to Randy than what he shows in the ring. Test your Randy Orton knowledge with some trivia.

ORTON TRIVIA

Q: Who was Randy's first TV match against?

A: Billy Gunn in an edition of Sunday Night HEAT

ORTON TRIVIA

Q: If Randy had not become a pro wrestler, what other profession did he want to be?

A: a movie stuntman

DID YOU KNOW...

Randy wasn't thinking only about his future career in pro wrestling during his time in school. He was also paying attention in class and studying. Randy was a straight 'A' student.

ORTON TRIVIA

Q: Who was Randy's favorite pro wrestler when he was growing up (other than family members)?

A: Jake "the Snake" Roberts

DID YOU KNOW...

Randy and many of his fellow wrestlers have spent much time performing in Europe. But Randy also joined them on a tour of Japan in 2006. In Japan pro wrestling is called "puroresu." The sport peaked in popularity in the 1960s and 1970s there. But it still has a strong following today.

ORTON TRIVIA

Q: What is Randy's favorite sandwich?

A: The Rueben sandwich—it has hot corned beef, melted Swiss cheese, and sauerkraut on rye bread.

Randy doesn't just perform in the ring. He sharpened his acting skills in a 2011 movie titled *That's What I Am*. Randy played the father of a bully. Film critic Lael Lowenstein called his performance "pitch perfect."

Randy's popularity has been used to sell many products. One memorable TV commercial that he did was for Kmart. In it, a family is sitting down to dinner. The mother scolds her young son, telling him that action figures are not allowed at the dinner table. The viewer expects to see a small toy action figure. Instead, the camera pans over to show the real-life Randy Orton!

VIRTUAL RANDY

Video game company THQ sometimes took digital photos of Randy during tapings of *Monday Night Raw*. They included various shots of Randy from different parts of his body. Why? So THQ producers could create a realistic Randy for their *WWE All Stars* video game, which was released in 2011.

Randy Orton has worked hard to be the best he can be in every aspect of his life. What does the future hold for Randy? With a winning attitude, a successful wrestling career, and a supportive family, the possibilities are endless.

GLOSSARY

AWOL (AY-wahl)—to leave or be absent from one's military duties without permission

babyface (BAY-bee-fayss)—a wrestler who acts as a hero in the ring

concussion (kuhn-KUH-shuhn)—an injury to the brain caused by a hard blow to the head

debut (day-BYOO)—a person's first public appearance

diva (DEE-vuh)—a female pro wrestler who may also accompany a male wrestler into the ring

feud (FYOOD)—to have a long-running quarrel between two people or groups of people

heel (HEEL)—a wrestler who acts as a villain in the ring

horizontal (hor-uh-ZON-tuhl)—flat and parallel to the ground

mixed martial arts (MIXT MAR-shuhl ARTS)—a full-combat sport combining wrestling and martial arts moves

stable (STAY-buhl)—a group of wrestlers who protect each other during matches and sometimes wrestle together

READ MORE

Jones, Patrick. *The Main Event: the Moves and Muscle of Pro Wrestling.* Minneapolis, Minn.: Millbrook Press, 2013.

Kaelberer, Angie Peterson. *The Fabulous, Freaky, Unusual History of Pro Wrestling.* Unusual Histories. Mankato, Minn.: Capstone Press, 2011.

Nemeth, Jason D. *Randy Orton.* Stars of Pro Wrestling. Mankato, Minn.: Capstone Press, 2010.

INTERNET SITES

FactHound offers a safe, fun way to find Internet sites related to this book. All of the sites on FactHound have been researched by our staff.

Here's all you do:

Visit *www.facthound.com*

Enter this code: 9781429686754

INDEX